82-1-2

DESIGNS OF CHINESE INDIGO BATIK

DESIGNS OF CHINESE INDIGO BATIK

by Lu Pu

With drawings and photographs by the author.

PREFACE by Jean Mailey
INTRODUCTION by Zhang Ding

Jointly Published by
LEE PUBLISHERS GROUP, INC., NEW YORK
and
NEW WORLD PRESS, BEIJING

Copyright © 1981 The New World Press, Beijing, China

LEE PUBLISHERS GROUP, INC.
745 Fifth Avenue, New York
New York, 10151

NEW WORLD PRESS
24, Bai Wan Zhuang,
Beijing, China

Library of Congress Cataloging in Publication Data

Lu, Pu, 1934-
    Designs of Chinese indigo batik.

    1. Batik—China—Themes, motives.   I. Title.
NK9503.L8   1981   746.6'62'0951   81-20832
ISBN 0-86519-014-3   AACR2

Designed by Irene Friedman

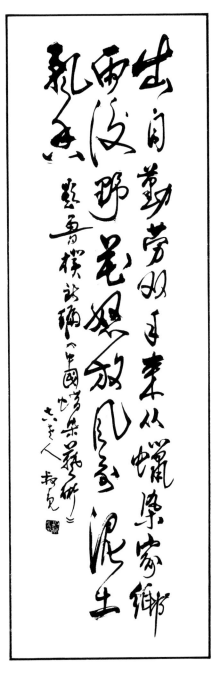

Created by nimble hands,
Coming from the home of indigo batik,
Like the wildflowers bursting forth after the rain,
Like the fragrance of the soil before the wind.
— Chen Shuliang

NOTE: The introductory poem and the calligraphy for the title were written by
the noted painter and calligrapher, Chen Shuliang, Vice-President
of the Central Academy of Arts and Crafts, Beijing.

CONTENTS

PREFACE

How fortunate that a Chinese artist, Lu Pu, has become interested in a special group of resist-printed folk textiles and the minority peoples living in the southwest provinces of China who make and use them. Distant from sophisticated centers, their handiwork reflects with vivid charm the lifestyle and beliefs of these little-known members of the vast Chinese nation. The only presently preserved material even remotely related to this seems to be the costumes of certain of the Miao groups decorated with geometrical details in indigo-resist dyeing and largely embroidered with cotton threads. Collected and studied by Carl Schuster, a group of these costumes are occasionally seen in natural history and anthropological museums.

Mr. Lu Pu presents here a selection of designs from his own large collection of fabrics gathered over several years, along with clear photographs and drawings. His text, most sympathetic and explicit, gives convincing details about the technique, a wax-resist process done with locally collected beeswax, somewhat related to that of the batiks of Java. His discussion refutes previous casual theories about rice paste as a universal resist agent in the hitherto little studied or collected indigo-resist country cottons of China.

These wax-resist dyed, home-woven bast fiber fabrics are used as dress materials, sleeve bands, sashes, shoes, door curtains, baby carriers, coverlets, valances — in fact, in connection with all aspects of life. In them appear lively and graceful birds and animals, imaginative plants and flowers which are sometimes combined with peonies, longevity emblems, cherry blossoms and pomegranates of traditional Chinese ornament reinterpreted with local zest. T-fret and S-scroll guard borders seen as early as Han pressed clay tomb tiles remind us how folk art sometimes preserves very ancient motifs indeed, while the frequent use of dotted guard borders and lines commented on by Lu Pu may represent a happy local addition. Some birds fly with spread wings and feet back over their heads in the traditional Chinese manner, while other birds seem to be turning into flowers as they fly. The frequent appearance of peacocks in various decorative forms reminds us that India is much nearer to these peoples than are the great cities of Chinese civilization.

Mr. Lu Pu, by appreciating, preserving and publishing this hitherto unknown folk art, has made a valuable contribution to art historians' study possibilities and to the pleasures of the sensitive eye as well.

Jean Mailey
Curator, Textile Study Room
The Metropolitan Museum of Art
New York
Spring 1981

China

HUANGPING •

DALI •

ANSHUN • DANZHAI •

LU'NAN •

THE PEOPLE'S
REPUBLIC OF CHINA

CHRONOLOGICAL CHART OF CHINESE DYNASTIES

Neolithic period	?? - 1766 B.C.
Shang	1766 - 1122 B.C.
Zhou	1122 - 770 B.C.
Spring and Autumn Annals	770 - 476 B.C.
Warring States	476 - 221 B.C.
Qin	221 - 206 B.C.
Han	206 B.C. - A.D. 220
Three Kingdoms	A.D. 220 - 265
Jin	A.D. 265 - 420
Southern and Northern	A.D. 420 - 589
Sui	A.D. 589 - 618
Tang	A.D. 618 - 907
Five Dynasties and Ten Kingdoms	A.D. 907 - 960
Song	
Northern Song	A.D. 960 - 1127
Southern Song	A.D. 1127 - 1279
Yuan	A.D. 1279 - 1368
Ming	A.D. 1368 - 1644
Qing	A.D. 1644 - 1911

INTRODUCTION

China has a recorded history of several thousand years. It is a country composed of many nationalities. Its vast and diverse folk art has for centuries contributed to the world's artistic development. The splendid Yangshao painted-pottery culture of the Neolithic period and the bronzes of the Shang and Zhou dynasties (1766 - 1122 B.C. and 1122 - 770 B.C. respectively) are both distinguished additions to the cultural wealth of mankind.

In examining Chinese folk art it may be helpful to compare it to the better known "palace art." Palace art was created for the palaces and pavilions of the Imperial Court during the long period of feudal society in China. The porcelain, cloisonné, lacquerware, silk embroidery, painting, and calligraphy reflect the lives of the intellectuals and rulers. It is essentially the classical art of the predominant Han nationality. Folk art, on the other hand, is created and enjoyed by the working people themselves and reflects their beliefs and ambitions. It often develops out of the necessities of the peoples' daily lives. Items are made of inexpensive local materials. Artisans rely heavily on local and regional traditions for patterns and techniques. Dolls and kites, paper-cuts, bamboo work, pottery, weaving and batik are among the various forms of Chinese folk art that are still alive today.

Undoubtedly palace art represents a higher level of artistic refinement, especially in terms of its designs and patterns. Its chief artistic method was that of stylization, and through stylization it achieved a certain freedom and variety. But particularly during the last days of the feudal society its artistic forms became rigid and dull, and its styles degenerated into inflexible formulas. Palace art — some of the dyed textiles, the ceramics, lacquerware, carved ivory, cloisonné, and even some of the calligraphy and painting — became too narrowly uniform.

Strictly speaking, folk art is not fully mature. Sometimes it is even rather coarse. On the other hand, it is always fresh, free and lively. Personally, I would always prefer a piece of folk blue-and-white printed cloth to a piece of palace satin adorned with designs of dragon roundels. Perhaps it is a matter of different aesthetic standards. Some people are fond of the mature fruit, others of the half ripe, and still others delight in the sharp flavors of the young fruit.

Folk art is closely linked to the daily lives of the people who create it. The designs adopted by the minority peoples are usually drawn from the environment around them. Their motifs are based upon the familiar plants and animals they see every day. Elephants and peacocks, for example, are common in the designs of the minorities living close to the subtropical zone, while other minorities use chickens, fish, birds and local flowers in their work. The ideals and feelings expressed in folk art are those celebrating love or praising life. They are simple but attractive and are quite different from the themes of palace art, which glorify Imperial authority by using such images as dragons, phoenixes, lions and tigers, or express yearnings for longevity and wealth by using such symbols as pine trees and cranes.

Indigo batik is mainly a folk art of China's national minority peoples. It is found in many regions, but it is chiefly concentrated in the remote southwestern provinces of Guizhou and Yunnan. The women of the minority peoples, including the Miao of Guizhou province and the Bai and Yi of Yunnan province, learn embroidery and batik in childhood from their mothers and grandmothers. During her youth, a girl will produce large numbers of batik garments to be used as her dowry. When she falls in love, batik ribbons are the first gift she will give to the boy as a sign of her affection. The youngsters joyfully use such ribbons as waistbands or braid them onto reed pipes. The beautiful blue-and-white batiks flutter and swirl as the young people play their musical instruments and join in lively dances. When the girl marries, her dowry of batik dresses and skirts fills many cases. The quality of the dowry is the product of the talent and skill of the young bride herself, and it reflects years of her strenuous efforts to develop her creative abilities.

Such social customs show just how indispensable a part of everyday life batik has become for the minority peoples. They use batik for all the daily necessities. Batik designs decorate satchels, kerchiefs, backpacks for carrying children, hats, shoes, swaddling bands, bedsheets, quilts, window curtains, handkerchiefs, and even the covers for the cages of pet thrushes. This rich variety of batik products eloquently expresses the talents of the craftswomen who create them and shows how integral a part batik plays in the peoples' daily lives. It is no wonder that the art of indigo batik has developed to a very high level.

The unique character of indigo batik is created not only by its relationship to the lives of its creators, but also by the materials and techniques the folk artists use in executing their designs. Forms are drawn on the plain white cloth with lines of varying density and dots of different sizes. The use of wax and smooth-edged wax knives for drawing makes the art of indigo batik entirely different from embroidery or from other methods of fabric dyeing and printing. In the production of blue-and-white printed cloth by the people of the Han nationality, for example, the method of making the pattern is quite different. Holes are punched into a cardboard pattern and the edges of the lines on the finished work have many sharp corners and angles, rather like the style of paper-cuts.

The indigo used as the dye in batik work is made from local plants. Its color is pure and deep and bright. The blue background and the designs formed by the white lines and dots provide a rich and satisfying variety. The undyed fabric remains clear white, though there are fine blue lines in the white, a characteristic feature of batik. These "ice lines" are created by cracks in the wax through which the blue dye seeps during the dyeing process, and they help give the batik its unity and coherence. Just like the simple bamboo flutes of Chinese music, the folk batiks achieve a rich beauty that is unique in texture.

Reference to the art of batik is found in the historical records of the Han and Tang dynasties (206 B.C - A.D. 220 and A.D. 618 - 907) respectively and batik dating from the Tang dynasty has been preserved in Japan. Today, however, most Chinese people know little or nothing of this art form. I would like to take this opportunity to express my heartfelt gratitude to author Lu Pu and others like him who are engaged in researching and recording the various forms of folk art. Lu Pu has spent many years collecting and studying large numbers of batik designs during his extensive travels in the remote minority re-gions of Guizhou and Yunnan. The de-signs presented in this book are among the best of his vast collection. This bright jewel of China's folk art might have been left behind in the mountains and valleys, unknown to the Chinese themselves and to the outside world, had it not been for his efforts. In fact, were it not for the work of artists and scholars who devote their time to the study of the arts and crafts of the people, treasures like these might dis-appear completely with the passage of time.

China's folk art is a great artistic re-source for all cultures. This volume will play a significant role in preserving the great traditional folk art of indigo batik. It will stimulate further research and collec-tion. It will also provide a unique inspira-tion and reference, not only to students of the arts and crafts in China, but to peoples throughout the world.

Zhang Ding
President, Central College
of Arts and Crafts
Beijing
Spring 1981

CHINESE INDIGO BATIK:
A FOLK ART

The National Minorities

China is the most populous nation on earth, with a total of over 900 million people. It is a republic made up of many national and ethnic groups. About ninety-four percent of the Chinese are from the Han group. However, there are about fifty-five non-Han ethnic groups in China. These people are known in China as the "national minorities."

Most of the minority peoples live in compact communities on the borders of Chinese territories - in the mountains, steppes and grasslands. Many of them have been influenced by Han culture over thousands of years of interaction, and they have contributed to the development of Chinese culture as a whole. Yet because of differences in their social customs and natural environments, many have maintained their individual cultural traditions.

The minority groups of the southwestern Chinese provinces of Guizhou and Yun-nan (about half of all the recognized minorities in China are located in the latter province) are fairly different from the Han Chinese. Living mostly in inaccessible mountainous terrain, the local people have developed a distinctive batik art. It is in these areas that I studied the styles and techniques of this indigenous folk art.

This volume contains a selection of 110 of the best batik designs from the extensive collection I have been able to build up during four visits in recent years to Guizhou and Yunnan. During my visits I went to famous centers of batik production and talked to many of the highly-skilled folk artists. I was able to examine innumerable pieces of batik preserved by the people, and even came across a lively apron design which is more than one hundred years old and which was shown to me by an elderly woman of eighty years of age who had inherited it from her parents (Pl. 78.)

The art of Chinese batik is an ancient folk art with a long history. It is still popular

Figure 1
A skillful batik designer of the Miao nationality in Guizhou province

in the regions of southwest China inhabited by minority peoples. Carrying on skills handed down from generation to generation, the Miao, Buyi, Gelao, Shui, Tu, Yi, Bai and Naxi minorities in the provinces of Guizhou and Yunnan have over a long period of time brought their art to a high level of refinement. Their batik designs cover a wide range of themes and are vividly expressed in bold line drawings. Their rich compositions and varied styles reflect their daily lives and their distinct local environments. The beauty and en-

chantment of this art never fails to capture the attention of students of the folk arts such as myself.

The History of Chinese Batik

Chinese batik has a history of more than 2000 years. Along with tie-dyeing and clamping between wooden blocks, it was one of the three major forms of resist dyeing in ancient times. Blue-and-white batik first appeared during the Han

Figure 2
Batiks from the Han dynasty (206 B.C. - A.D. 220)
have been discovered in ancient tombs.
The cloth fragments reveal white flowers made
of a central dot surrounded by
smaller dots on a bright blue ground.
The flowers are separated by lines
of dots forming rhomboids.

Figure 3
Tree, elephant and sheep designs on a batik sceen
from the Tang dynasty (A.D. 618 - 907)

Figure 4
Batik plays a vital role in the everyday life and culture of the
minority peoples of southwestern China. Here, Miao
women exchange ideas as they work outside their homes.

Figure 5
A batik dress

dynasty (206 B.C. - A.D. 220). Unearthed in an ancient tomb in Turpan County, in Xinjiang, the batiks show small white flower designs on a bright blue background. Each flower is made of a central white dot surrounded by smaller dots; the flowers are separated by straight rows of dots forming rhomboids (Fig. 2).

Blue-and-white batik was widely produced in the Tang dynasty (A.D. 618 - 907), when it was used on men's and women's clothing. Multicolored batik was also produced. In addition to small flower designs used for dress material, large pictures of trees, birds, animals and landscapes were made for use as room screens. Such materials were quite exquisite. The products were shipped for sale to Japan and southeast Asia. Some of the Tang dynasty batiks preserved in the Masakura-In collection in Japan were done on thin gauze (Fig. 3).

According to the historical record *Report From Beyond the Southern Hills (Ling Wai Dai Da)* of the Southern Song dynasty (A.D. 1127 - 1279), the "Yao people produce very fine designs on blue cloth. The method of production is that the designs are engraved on two wooden boards, between which the cloth is sandwiched. Then, the grooves are filled with beeswax, and the cloth is released from the boards. The wax is removed after the dyeing process. Very delicate designs appear on the cloth." From this it can be seen that batik was produced on a large scale in Song times. During the Yuan and Ming dynasties (A.D. 1279 - 1368 and A.D. 1368 - 1644 respectively), designs developed into several fixed styles.

After the introduction of mechanized printing and dyeing techniques and imported piece goods, hand printing and dyeing methods gradually died out in most parts of the country. In the remote border regions of Guizhou and Yunnan, however, the techniques of wax-resist dyeing not only have continued, they have flourished.

Today batik is studied by individual artists and by Chinese arts and crafts institutions so that this rich and unique design legacy, alive and thriving for over 2000 years, will be preserved for future generations.

Batik: A Cultural Tradition

The craft of batik production in Guizhou and Yunnan satisfies practical needs of the people and at the same time embellishes and enriches their lives. The women particularly love beauty and pay great attention to the way they dress. From a young age, they study the techniques of making batik under the guidance of their mothers and grandmothers. As their skills develop, batik designs are used to adorn their garments (Fig. 5), bedding, knapsacks, bags and kerchiefs. They even use batik on their shoes and on cloths for

Figure 6
Batik wrapping cloths in use

Figure 7
Dancing around the "tree of longevity" at the annual Spring Festival

Figure 8
A woman offering a man a batik ribbon as a token of her love

Figure 9
During festivals, women wear colorful batik dresses and men play reed pipes.

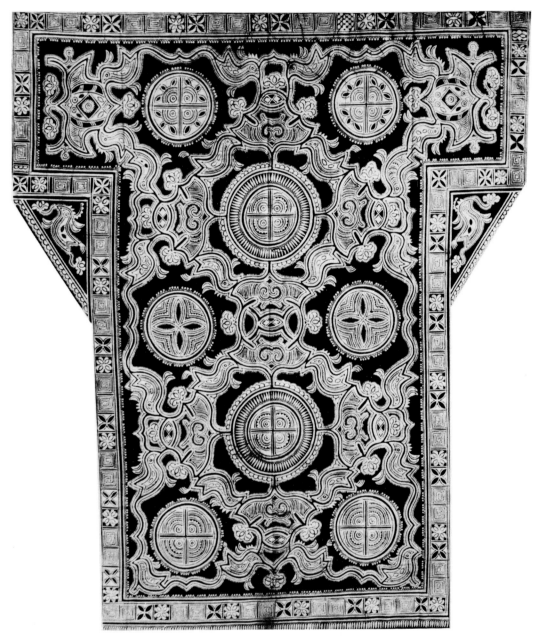

Figure 10
Minority people pay particular attention to the
symbolic designs they use on backcloths
for carrying their babies. The stunning example
above has motifs that predict longevity,
prosperity and happiness for the child.

wrapping parcels (Fig. 6). In some instances, a particularly beautiful batik wrapping cloth is hung on the wall as a decoration. The girls constantly examine each other's work and exchange ideas. Fairs and dancing grounds turn into "shows" where they can view each other's batik designs and exchange tips on batik techniques.

At the time of the Spring Festival, when new growth shows on the trees and the flowers blossom, the traditional dancing grounds are opened. The minority peoples assemble there from the surrounding areas and join in the celebrations. The girls wear colorful batik dresses and dance around the "tree of longevity" with boys who play reed pipes. Each year before the dances, an evergreen tree is felled and planted in the center of the dancing ground as a symbol of longevity. After the dance meeting, a childless couple may take the tree home and place it across a roof beam of their home to signify the "entry of life" into their house. At the Spring Festival in the following year, a family which has had a child presents a new evergreen tree to the dancing ground. As the singing and dancing progress, girls give carefully crafted batik ribbons to the young men with whom they have fallen in love. The ribbons are tied onto the reed pipes as a token of the bond formed between the couple (Figs. 7, 8, 9). On moonlit nights, the young men can recognize their sweethearts in the shade of the trees on the hillsides by the different identifying batik designs on their skirts.

The pieces of batik made by the young girls as they grow up are kept to form their dowries. As a girl develops a relationship with a young man, she makes his satchels, bags and parcel wrapping cloths. On the day of the marriage the girl's family has to send trunks of batik clothing to the home of the bridegroom. After childbirth, the infant's grandmother on the mother's side has to present a cloth with an auspicious design on it to

Figure 11
Using a backcloth to carry a baby

24

Figure 12
Design from a backcloth used for carrying a baby.
Here, pomegranate, peach, *shou* and *panchang* infuse the cloth with
an auspicious meaning. Because the pomegranate has many seeds, it has
traditionally symbolized "many children," and in Chinese folk
tradition the peach is the fruit of the immortals,
thus suggesting wishes for longevity.

Figure 13
Butterflies and blossoming flowers
are commonly used motifs in Anshun, where
the drawing style is naturalistic.

Figure 14
In Huangping in Guizhou province, batik
designs are laid out in a regular and balanced
manner, and motifs are often stylized.
The nonrepresentational pattern above shows three
birds flying around a central flower.

be used for carrying the child on the back (Figs. 10, 11, 12). If the father-in-law of the bride loves to keep birds, the new daughter-in-law has to provide batik covers for the cages. No wonder girls before marriage devote much of their time and energy to making batik articles! Their work is imbued with their hopes and desires for a happy life and full of their ideals and their love of beauty.

Girls skilled in making batiks are ardently sought after by suitors. Their abilities are seen as an expression of their talents and value. Consequently, a mother begins teaching her daughter the art of batik as soon as the child reaches the age of seven or eight. The most skillful producers of batik are folk artists who have been studying their craft from childhood. The abundance of batik articles represents a wealth of artistic experience gathered over many years. Southwestern China, the land of batik, is thus the home of a rich and beautiful artistic tradition passed on from generation to generation.

Surrounded by great natural beauty, the women draw· upon the familiar and beloved wildflowers and plants of the hills, the birds in the trees and the fish in the streams as the basis for their batik designs. They use such images to express their feelings, their imaginations and their wishes. Over the years a basic common style has evolved which is direct and lively, with an elegant delineation of form, a simplicity of presentation and a refined method of boldly depicting and interpreting their surroundings. The artistic value of batik thus lies not only in the loveliness of its forms, but also in its lyrical expression of the joy of life. Along with their oral literature and mountain songs, it conveys the simple beauty of the culture of the minority peoples.

CHARACTERISTIC STYLES AND MOTIFS

The environments, habits and customs of each minority are different, and as a

Figure 15
Typical stylized bird motifs of the Huangping region. (The uppermost abstract bird form is taken from the design shown in Figure 14.)

Figure 16
Fish motifs appear in the batik designs
from Danzhai, a low lying area of
lush river valleys.

Figure 17
The artists from Dali in Yunnan
province frequently depict roosters
and chickens.

Figure 18
Lu'nan in Yunnan province has
a subtropical climate where exotic
animals and birds thrive.
Elephants and peacocks appear in
the art of the region.

Figure 12
Many of the areas in southwestern China are places of great scenic splendor, and the local
artists draw inspiration for their designs from the natural beauty surrounding them.
Here, Miao women wash batiks near a magnificent waterfall.

result the batiks of each minority and each district have their own characteristics.

Anshun in Guizhou province, where members of the Miao nationality live, lies on a plain. Blossoms, butterflies and birds are common subjects for the batik designs, which are executed in a lively, realistic and unrestrained style (Fig. 13; Pls. 6 to 45).

Huangping in Guizhou, also a Miao district, is a mountainous forest area. The birds that thrive in the forests are a major theme of the batik designs, which are laid out in a regular and balanced manner. Motifs are often stylized and forms distorted (Figs. 14, 15; Pls. 46 to 54).

By contrast, the Miaos living along the lush river valleys of Danzhai base their designs on birds, flowers, fish and butterflies. Peaches and pomegranates also appear frequently. Bold, flowing lines are used, and compositions are full and rich (Fig. 16; Pls. 55 to 77).

In Dali in Yunnan province, the batik designs of the Tu, Yi and Bai nationalities are usually combined with embroidery. Living in a lush, subtropical zone, the designers choose chickens, flowers, monkeys and rats as the subjects for their batiks (Fig. 17; Pls. 78 to 97).

The Naxi, Miao and Yi nationalities of Lu'nan, also in Yunnan province, live in an area of great scenic splendor known as "The Stone Forest." Here, strangely-

Figure 20
The Chinese characters
shou (long life) and
panchang (good fortune without limit)
often appear in the folk batiks,
either as a decorative border or as
part of the main design.

Figure 21
Design from a backcloth used
for carrying a baby

Figure 19
Since fish lay many eggs, they are
used to symbolize fecundity,
prosperity and affluence.

shaped rock formations are reflected in mountain lakes, and there are high waterfalls and dense forests. Many Chinese legends explain the origin of the lofty stone pillars of the region, and the local batik artists use themes from these folk tales as well as representations of human figures, peacocks and elephants in their designs (Fig. 18; Pls. 98 to 110).

SYMBOLISM

Many of the traditional motifs for the batik designs of the minority peoples have special meanings. Fish, for example, are used in a number of contexts. Because they produce many eggs, they are

30

taken as a symbol of guaranteed succession through many generations, thereby implying that the minority people will flourish (Fig. 19). A fishing hook is a symbol of a girl's hope that she will find a suitor. Fish depend on water and this relationship is meant to symbolize love and affection between a man and woman, an idea that is expressed in the following folk song from Anshun:

Beneath the rock bursts forth a precious stream,

Deep below where reaches not the morning beam.

Like a thirsty rhinoceros comes my sweet,

While I, like a carp, rush him to meet.

The Miao women of Danzhai frequently use the Chinese characters *shou* (long life) and *panchang* (good fortune without limit) as motifs in their batiks in the hope that they will bring good luck, prosperity and longevity (Fig. 20; Pls. 57, 60, 67).

Peaches, pomegranates and peonies appear in the batik designs. For the Chinese they are rich with symbolic associations. Peaches symbolize long life because in the folk tradition they are the fruit of the immortals. They also represent marriage and springtime. Pomegranates

Figure 23
A whirlpool design from a Yangshao painted vase.

have many seeds, and thus they are used to symbolize posterity and abundant offspring (Fig. 21; Pl. 66). Peonies represent spring, prosperity, love and affection, and feminine beauty (Pl. 11).

The people of the Miao and Shui minorities use a spiral-shaped design in a broad band around their collars and cuffs. In Miao this is known as the *wotuo* (Fig. 22; Pl. 69). The total design has eight circles made up of four on each sleeve. When the sleeves are held together, the design is complete. There are several traditional explanations for this design. One version claims that once there was a clever and talented young Miao girl who was skilled at batik. She fell seriously ill and didn't get better no matter what medicine she took. One day her mother, who was washing on a hill slope, came across a fresh patch of herbal moss. She

Figure 22
The traditional *wotuo* design is worn on sleeves and collars.

31

Figure 24
Line drawing designs of phoenixes and
clouds from laquerware of the
Warring States period (476 - 221 B.C.)

Figure 25
This line drawing of a phoenix is
from a painted brick of the
Han dynasty (206 B.C. - A.D. 220).

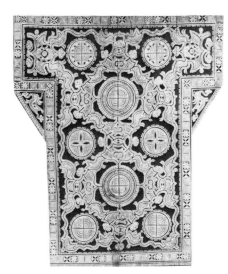

Figure 10
A backcloth for carrying a baby

Figure 26
Regular repetition of graphic elements, such as large motifs or small dots and curved lines, is a characteristic device of the batik artists.

Figure 27
Note the harmonious, decorative effect achieved by the regular repetition of dots between lines.

fed it to her daughter, who quickly recovered. As an expression of her eternal gratitude, the girl developed a design to resemble the shape of the moss, thus starting the tradition. Another story states that when making solemn sacrifices to their ancestors, the Miao had a tradition of killing an ox. The woman used the spiral pattern on top of the ox's head as a design for their clothing to show reverence for their ancestors. Whatever the real origin, this design has been continuously handed down and cannot be freely altered.

The art of batik is full of life and local color. As society develops and contacts between peoples expand, the women absorb new influence into their batik art and constantly develop new themes and styles.

Batik: A Decorative Art

The Chinese tradition of decorative art goes back to the Neolithic era, when the surface of the Yangshao pottery was decorated with paint (Fig. 23). Decorative art is primarily ornamental. It neither adds to the usefulness of a piece nor is restricted in design by the prerequisites of association with ritual. It aims to please the eye, to create an interesting pattern. Designs are frequently based on regular repetitions of graphic elements, and they are often integrally related to the forms they embellish. The many different styles of batik art conform to these prescriptions, and thus stand proudly among the achievements of the decorative arts and crafts of China.

33

Figure 28
The antennae of this butterfly
are exaggerated for decorative purposes.

Figure 14
Huangping batik

USE OF LINE

The art of batik is a simple one of white designs on a blue ground. Line drawing is the major means of expression, and careful attention is paid to the shapes of the background areas between the lines.

Lines are drawn with ease, grace and variety, creating beautiful harmonies and rhythms. The lines give the forms a feeling of movement and life, for there is an organic relationship between the speed and force with which the lines are placed onto the fabric and the vitality and spirit of the final batik (Pls. 26, 71).

Batik has inherited the traditional line drawing methods of the Chinese arts. Exquisite line drawing was used on the Yangshao painted pottery. Later the development of line drawing techniques was apparent on the lacquerware of the Warring States period (476 - 221 B.C.; Fig. 24) on painted bricks of the Han dynasty (206 B.C. - A.D. 220; Fig. 25), and on the Dunhuang cave murals. The result of drawing designs on cloth with knives and wax is much the same as that achieved by drawing with brushes and paint.

Repetition

Regular repetition and organized variation of graphic elements builds up patterns in the batik designs. Both small components (such as dots and short lines) and larger ones (such as graphic motifs or geometric shapes) are repeated to enhance the decorative effect. The finished batik is held together by an overall sense of harmony, rhythm, movement and balance (Figs. 26, 27, 10; Pls. 44, 80).

Stylization

The batik artists use stylization primarily to serve the artistic demands of their designs. The distorted and stylized forms create starkly effective graphic images (Pl. 77). The antennae of a butterfly (Fig. 28; Pls. 28, 93), the stem of a flower (Pl. 36) or the wings of a bird (Pl. 58) may be exaggerated for compositional and rhythmic purposes, or an abstract pattern may be made of repeated stylized animal shapes (Fig. 14; Pl. 53).

Images are sometimes distorted to serve symbolic and imaginative purposes

Figure 29
Forms are occasionally distorted for symbolic reasons. This design of flowers within flowers is meant to show the abundance of the beauty of life.

Figure 30
Flower petals drawn as birds' heads suggest the unity of all living things.

Figure 31
An example of imaginative freedom: the wings of a bird are drawn as those of a butterfly.

as well. To represent a profusion of blossoms and beauty, designs show flowers blooming within flowers (Fig. 29; Pl. 21). All the parts of a flower might be shown in order to emphasize its sturdiness (Pl. 27). A flower might be drawn in the shape of a fish, and flower petals might be depicted by using butterfly wings or birds' heads (Fig. 30, Pl. 18, 19). A fantastic creature might be invented by drawing the wings of a butterfly or the parts of a flower onto the body of a bird (Fig. 31; Pls. 16, 37, 62).

Such exaggeration and distortion of outward reality, linking flower, butterfly, bird and fish motifs, shows the great imaginative freedom of the folk artists and demonstrates their rich love of life. It also aptly reflects the lush landscapes that surround them and from which they draw their artistic inspiration.

COMPOSITION

The skills and talents of the folk artists are fully expressed in the richness and variety of the compositions they use in their batik designs.

Many of the compositions have decorative borders. The border outlines a specific space, thus defining the size and shape of the field upon which the design will be painted. A variety of border shapes are used: squares, circles, rectangles, semicircles, ovals, rhomboids, or free-flowing shapes that follow the outlines of a garment such as an apron, waistband, sleeve or cap (Pls. 15, 87, 92). Frequently the folk artists place a round motif within a square space or vice versa (Fig. 32; Pls. 43, 49). The border becomes a graphic device itself, relating to the other elements in the design and helping to create the sense of pictorial organization. A border may be either a simple line or an elaborately patterned band of many small elements.

Open compositions, where only the edges of the fabric being painted upon define the pictorial shape and the field for decoration, are another frequently used compositional style. This type of composition often appears on large fabrics such as quilts, bedsheets and wrapping cloths. Flowers, butterflies, birds and fish are drawn in a relaxed and flowing manner. The designs are loose, free, airy and expansive (Fig. 33; Pls. 35, 38, 102).

Nearly all the compositions of the batik artists stress harmony and balance. Pictorial elements are placed to correspond in size, shape and position. The exact same fish or flower motif may be repeated to create a symmetrical design (Pl. 46), or a well-balanced composition will allow for some variation in the parts (Fig. 34; Pl. 10, 27). A large central flower might be surrounded by several smaller flowers, each different from the next, but despite the irregularities in form and spacing, the composition will be kept balanced and in proportion (Pl. 91).

The placement of the pictorial elements in the batik designs is not only governed by concern for harmony and balance, but also by the traditional Chinese preference for decorative elaboration and enriched surface pattern. Many of the batik designs rely upon the careful placement of multiple elements of different sizes. While at first glance a principal motif may appear to be one flower, study shows it to be a neat and orderly layout of many flowers of various sizes, with the space around the larger figures filled with many tiny flower shapes (Fig. 35). In other designs one motif will predominate, but it will be supported by several designs of secondary importance (Pl. 25).

Interestingly, in the indigo batiks of southwestern China, compositions using one single dominant motif with very little background decoration can be found (Pls. 20, 55, 107), as can compositions with pictorial elements in scattered positions in nonbalanced designs (Pl. 64). The rich variety of this folk art form shows it has not only succeeded to the artistic traditions of China, it has also made outstanding contributions of its own.

Figure 32
Batik designs often have decorative borders, and frequently the folk artists place a round motif within a square frame.

Figure 33
Open compositions, where only the edges of the fabric being
painted upon define the field for decoration, are
a common compositional style.

Figure 34
A floral design that allows for variation
in the parts yet remains well balanced

Figure 35
A balanced composition with many different-size elements skillfully distributed

THE TECHNIQUE OF PRODUCING CHINESE INDIGO BATIK

Batik wax-resist dyeing is so named because wax is used as an agent to resist the dye applied to a piece of cloth, thereby creating a pattern. As recorded in the *Guizhou Tongzhi* (or *Annals of Guizhou*), a local historical record of the geography, economy, customs and culture of the area, "Wax is used for drawing designs on cloth before dyeing. After the dyeing process when the wax is removed, the designs are as distinct as if they had been painted." Producers of batik draw designs on cloth with copper knives dipped into molten wax. As the wax solidifies, delicate broken lines appear on its surface. When the waxed cloth is put into a vat of indigo blue dye, the parts covered with wax remain white. Because the liquid dye penetrates the cracks in the wax, however, fine "ice lines" appear in the pattern, giving batik a unique characteristic and adding to the artistic effect

(Fig. 36). After the wax is removed with boiling water, the printed material is washed and the complete batik reveals its beautiful blue-and-white designs.

Tools and Materials

Still employing techniques developed long ago, the peoples of Guizhou and Yunnan produce batiks using cloth they weave themselves on simple looms, dyes they make themselves from local plants, and yellow wax they obtain from their own beehives. The raw materials are readily available and the creative techniques are simple, so the production of batik is widespread and easy.

Below is a list of the tools and materials used for producing Chinese indigo batik:

- Bleached cloth
- Paste starch. The tuber of taro is

Figure 36
Thin "ice lines" in the white portion of the design are a distinguishing
trait of batik. They are created during the dyeing process when
the liquid dye seeps through fine cracks in the wax.

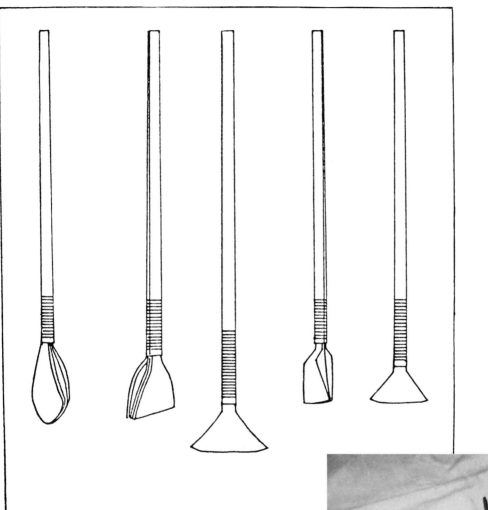

made into a paste starch used to stiffen the fabric before the drawing with wax begins.

- Knives. Several different-shaped knives are used to apply the wax (Fig. 37). These knives are made from two or more pieces of copper with spaces left between them to carry a charge of wax. They are rather axelike in appearance. The copper pieces measure about one centimeter (about half an inch wide) and when fixed on to a wooden handle make a knife about eight centimeters (four inches long). Since the copper retains heat, the charge of wax flows easily when the pattern is drawn.

Figure 37
Copper wax knives

● Beeswax and paraffin wax. Beeswax is a secretion from worker bees used for making honeycomb. It is insoluble in water. Its melting point is 62° to 66° C (144° to 151° F). Paraffin wax is less pliable than beeswax. The two types of wax are mixed in proportions that differ in different localities — sometimes half each and sometimes two-thirds beeswax to one-third paraffin wax. The proportion depends upon the intent of the designer and the quality of the cloth being used. If the material is comparatively thick and absorbent, then more paraffin wax is used because it is brittle and cracks easily, thus creating the desired "ice lines."

The temperature of the wax also affects the end result. If the temperature is too high, the wax soaks into the cloth, making clear outlines impossible. If the temperature is too low, the wax sticks to the knife and does not flow.

● Indigo blue dye. This is a natural dyestuff made from the fermented leaves of *polygonum tinctorium*, an annual herbaceous plant belonging to the *polygonaceae* family (Fig. 38). It has long oval leaves that grow in pairs. It blossoms in July and is harvested in August.

In the *Compendium of Materia Medica* compiled by Li Shizhen of the Ming dynasty (A.D. 1368 - 1644), it is recorded that "In the south, the people dig pits to soak the indigo leaves and stir in the lime. When the mixture has settled and the lime has penetrated the leaves, the water is removed and the residue is used as indigo for dying." The minority peoples of Guizhou and Yunnan still use this ancient method to produce their dye.

● Additional materials include: ox bones, used to press the starched cloth flat and smooth; bamboo sections, used to draw circles; and earthenware bowls, used to hold the molten wax over the burning charcoal (Figs. 39, 40, 41).

Figure 38
The leaves of the *polygonum tinctorium* plant are fermented to make indigo blue dye.

The Process of Making Batik

The specific techniques for making batik vary slightly from area to area, but the basic process remains the same: first the cloth is cleaned and treated to ensure the adhesion of the molten wax and the penetration of the dyestuff; next the layout of the design is marked on the cloth; and finally, the cloth is waxed and dyed.

The Miao of the Huangping region prepare the cloth by boiling it for twenty minutes in water containing caustic soda to free the fabric of foreign substances. Paste starch, made by boiling the tuber of taro, is applied to the cloth, which is then pinned to a piece of flat wood to make it taut. In other localities the cloth is not starched, but is simply fixed to a wooden board with paraffin wax. In the Danzhai area, the Miao people starch the cloth and then rub it with an ox bone to give the material a smooth, shiny surface. The batik artist then simply holds the stiffened cloth on her lap while working.

After the cloth is prepared, the layout is planned using rice stalks of different lengths as rulers (Figs. 42, 43). The proper

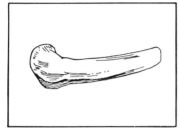

Figure 39
Ox bone, used to press
the starched cloth
flat and smooth

Figure 40
Bamboo sections, used
to draw circles

Figure 41
Earthenware bowls, used
to hold the molten wax over
burning charcoal

Figure 42
The layout of the design is planned
on the cloth before the actual
drawing with wax begins. Here, the
artist holds the cloth on her lap.

distribution of the motifs and proportions of the design are decided upon, and the layout is indicated on the cloth with small marks made by the thumbnail. Then the design is drawn on the cloth using the knives charged with molten wax (Fig. 44).

When the wax dries, the cloth is put into a vat filled with indigo blue for ten to fifteen minutes (Fig. 45). Afterward, it is hung in the open air to oxidize. The first dyeing yields a light blue color. The dyeing process is repeated and the color deepens to a darker blue. The number of times the cloth is dyed depends upon the depth of color desired.

After drying, the dyed cloth is placed into boiling water to remove the wax (Fig. 46). Once the wax is removed, the dyed cloth is washed in clean water to get rid of any surplus dye (Fig. 47). The batik is then ironed and the material is ready to be sewn into the desired product.

BATIK IN SEVERAL COLORS

Traditionally only dark blue dye was used for batik designs. More recently,

Figure 43
A woman marking out a batik design on stiffened cloth that has been fixed to a wooden board

Figure 44
The design is drawn using knives charged with molten wax.

Figure 45
Dipping the waxed cloth into a vat of indigo dye

Figure 46
The dyed cloth is placed
into boiling water to remove the wax.

Figure 47
Surplus dye is washed away in clean water.

Figure 48
Washing the finished batik article

however, batiks of several colors have been made.

If light and dark blue colors are to appear on the same piece of batik, the waxed cloth is dipped into the indigo vat until the proper light blue color is obtained. Then the cloth is hung and dried. The portion of the cloth that is to remain light blue is covered with wax to prevent further dyeing, and the fabric is returned to the vat for subsequent dyeings to produce a darker blue color. When the wax is removed, the light and dark blue areas are clearly distinct.

The minority peoples also make batiks in blue, red and yellow. They make red dye from the leaves of red bayberry and yellow dye from the leaves of *frandinus chinensis* or the seeds of *gardenia jasminoides* (Fig. 49).

There are two ways to make multicolor batiks. One is to dye the waxed cloth blue and then after it has dried and the wax has been removed, the other colors are dyed over the blue, leading to new color combinations. The other method is to first dye the fabric with red or yellow while the rest of the cloth is protected by wax. Then the wax is removed and new wax placed over the colored portions. The fabric is then dipped into the indigo vat. This method leads to pure, uncombined colors.

Figure 49
Gardenia jasminoides is an evergreen bush that blossoms in spring and summer and bears fragrant, white flowers. Yellow dye is obtained by soaking the fruit of this plant (upper right, above) in water.

AN ALBUM OF DESIGNS

On the following pages are over 110 batik designs that I collected in several trips to the remote provinces of southwestern China. This album is meant to be a source of pleasure and inspiration, as well as a permanent record of the remarkable artistic achievement of the peoples from Guizhou and Yunnan provinces. With few exceptions the designs as shown omit the fine ''ice lines'' that are characteristic of the finished batik pieces.

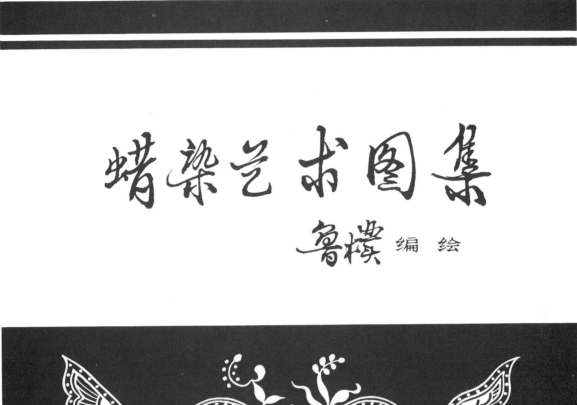

蜡染艺术图集

鲁樸 编绘

CREATIVE DESIGNS
BY THE AUTHOR

创新蜡染

This section contains five original designs by the author. They are based on the motifs and styles of the traditional folk batiks of the peoples of southwestern China.

Plate 1
Design for a Knapsack
This piece is based on batik designs collected in Yunnan
province. Two peacocks are flying among palm trees.
The ground is covered with flowers and butterflies.
The design was inspired by the beautiful natural scenery
of Jing Hong (Xishuangbanna), a nature preserve in
southern Yunnan. As is typical of many of the folk batiks,
dots are used extensively and the plant forms are
stylized to increase the decorative effect.

Plate 1

Plate 2
Design for a Knapsack
This is another piece derived from Yunnan batik.
A glorious peacock, spreading its wings and tail, is the focal point.
Geometric patterns are used to create a partial border.

Plate 2

Plate 3
Design for a Wrapping Cloth
Based on the art of the Miao people living in Anshun,
Guizhou province, this design shows four fish swimming
after one another. The batik expresses hopes for
a bountiful harvest and an affluent future.

Plate 3

Plate 4
Design for a Teapot Place Mat
In this design the central, unadorned background
provides a stark contrast to the complicated patterns on either
side. Butterflies and a pomegranate, symbols that often
appear in the folk batik pieces, comprise the central motif.
The lines are ornate and varied in thickness, and there is a
harmonious progression of repeated floral motifs.

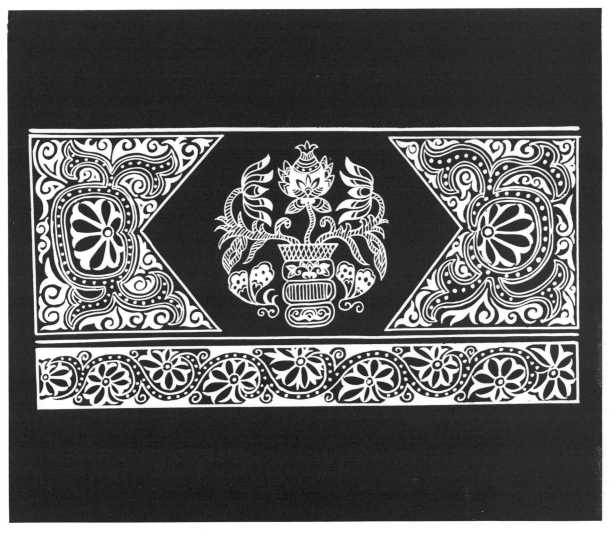

Plate 4

Plate 5
Design for a Wrapping Cloth
This symmetrical design depicts a scene in the spring.
The composition is orderly and balanced. The curved,
flowing lines of the plant stems are echoed by
the simple line of the square border.

Plate 5

DESIGNS FROM
ANSHUN, GUIZHOU PROVINCE

安顺蜡染

The batik designs in this section were done by the Miao peoples living in Anshun in Guizhou province. Anshun is located on a plain. Birds, flowers and fish are the major motifs. The drawing style is lively and naturalistic, and the compositions are varied.

Plate 6
Design From a Bag
A rich pattern is created here using only a few
simple dots and lines. The central motif shows a flower
in full bloom between two chirping birds. The
composition is balanced, and there are slight variations in
the details: compare the birds' beaks, tails and breast feathers,
for example. The design symbolizes the beauty of
the relationship between all living things.

Plate 6

Plate 7
Designs From Sleeve Trimmings
Birds, fish and peonies are typical motifs of
the batiks from Anshun province.

Plate 7

Plate 8
Designs From Waistband Trimmings
Both these designs are well balanced compositionally,
and both use line expressively. The jagged and billowing lines
of the flowers' leaves and petals help convey a
feeling of growth and upward movement.

Plate 8

Plate 9
Designs From Door Curtain Edgings
Top: Two goldfish nibble on a flower
Bottom: A flowing and expansive floral pattern

Plate 9

Plate 10
Designs From Door Curtain Edgings
Top: Bird and flower motifs of corresponding size are
placed opposite each other for balance. Notice how
vividly the birds are drawn. They appear to have just heard
a noise: one is alertly listening and the other seems
about to dart off in flight. Bottom: A floral design
that stresses compositional balance

Plate 10

Plate 11
Designs From Dress Material
Peonies, a traditional symbol of female beauty,
are used here on dress material.

Plate 11

Plate 12
Designs From Door Curtain Edgings
Sturdy, well-shaped pumpkins, and pumpkin
flowers in full bloom

Plate 12

Plate 13
Design From a Quilt Cover
Fish, birds, butterflies, peaches and flowers within flowers
suggest the unbounded beauty of spring.

Plate 13

Plate 14
Designs From a Backcloth Used for Carrying a Baby
Top: Two birds, combining features of peacocks
and golden pheasants, usher in the spring.
Bottom: Matching flower motifs

Plate 14

Plate 15
Design From a Waistband
Three graceful creatures, part bird and part fish, hold
floral sprays in their mouths. The shape outlined by the border
pattern is determined by the shape of the waistband.

Plate 15

Plate 16
Design From a Wrapping Cloth
This is an unusual and imaginative design. Its composition
is open and elements are scattered. The bird on the
left has butterfly wings, and it moves placidly in
an open and unadorned space. This contrasts sharply
with the bird on the right, who is surrounded by
turbulent movement. Its large tail streams
outward behind it as it swoops downward. Flowers issue
from its body and curl and flow around it.
The painting is lively and unrestrained. Here, the folk
artist has given free rein to her imagination.

84

Plate 16

Plate 17
Miscellaneous Flower Designs
Note the bird behind the flower on the lower left.

Plate 17

Plate 18
Designs From a Bib
Top: A single flower motif is boldly executed.
Bottom: Several of the flower's
petals look like birds' heads.

Plate 18   89

Plate 19
Designs From Sleeve Trimmings
Top: Three recurring motifs of Anshun batik — flowers,
butterflies and birds — are shown in this one design. Notice
the variety of line used to delineate the bird's tail: barbed,
thin lines and thick, gliding lines combine to suggest exotic
plumage. The bird is drawn singing vividly.
Bottom: Flower petals in the shape of birds' heads

Plate 19

Plate 20
Design From the Back of a Coat
A single flowing motif of great dramatic impact.
The large flower bears in its center a smaller one, signifying
the abundance of beauty and flowers.

Plate 20

93

Plate 21
Design From a Quilt Cover
Two pretty butterflies play with a flower in
a design symbolizing love and affection. As is
frequently the case with Chinese indigo batik, dots
act as a unifying design element.

Plate 21

Plate 22
Design From a Door Curtain
Two birds herald the birth of spring.
Compare with Plates 14 and 24.

Plate 22

Plates 23
Designs From Waistband Trimmings
Top: A fish, a bird and a flower in a rhythmic progression
Bottom: A decorative repeat pattern of floral motifs

Plate 23

Plate 24
Design From a Wrapping Cloth
A nonsymmetrical, well-balanced composition
showing a pair of birds and a pair of butterflies with
a flower, and a decorative border pattern

Plate 24

Plate 25
Design From a Wrapping Cloth
Here is an example of the typical batik compositional
technique of creating one large motif out of several smaller ones.
Four fish are looking for food amid four underwater plants.
The fish tails, each different from the other, fan out
gracefully and effortlessly. Note that the fish are shown
from above while the flowers are depicted in profile.

Plate 25

Plate 26
Design From a Door Curtain
This design is remarkable for the expressive quality
of the line. Two phoenixes in full flight are shown with a large
peony. The extraordinary freedom and power with which
the birds are drawn indicates the hand of a skilled and confident
artist. The organic relationship between the forcefulness
and vigor with which the wax lines were originally placed onto
the fabric and the vitality of the final image is undeniable.

Plate 26

Plate 27
Design From a Wrapping Cloth Edging
A repeat border patten, a flying bird, and a flower
in full bloom. The flower's petals, stamens and
pistils are all clearly shown.

Plate 27

Plate 28
Miscellaneous Designs
These examples of butterfly and fish designs are
taken from a variety of batik articles made by the Miao
people of Guizhou. The tendency to use exaggeration
of form is seen in the antennae of the
butterflies and the tails of the fish.

Plate 28

Plate 29
Designs From Sleeve Trimmings
Top: A flower balanced by a golden pheasant in flight
Bottom: Peonies blossoming fully and buds about to open

Plate 29

Plate 30
Design From a Kerchief
Twin birds perched on a branch with flowers.
One bird form overlaps the other,
giving a sense of depth to the image.

Plate 30

Plate 31
Design From a Door Curtain
An elaborate border of geometric shapes with bird and
flower motifs, and sturdy fish swimming under a large
flower with petals that look like birds

Plate 31

Plate 32
Designs From Sleeve Trimmings
Top: A delicate design of butterflies, fish
and flowers linked by a continuous scrolling line
Bottom: A bird and flower design

Plate 32

Plate 33
Design From a Kerchief
An open, well-balanced composition with one major
graphic element. Note the variety of line used to depict the bird
on the right, and the importance of the negative space
between the lines to the success of the image.

Plate 33

Plate 34
Design From a Wrapping Cloth
The balance between the fish and flowers of different
sizes in this graceful design displays the artist's fine sense of
proportion. Repeated dots and short lines create a rich pattern.
The border is a continuous repeat of fish and flower motifs.

Plate 34

Plate 35
Design From a Wrapping Cloth
This open and fluid design shows a peacock
playing with peonies, symbolizing deep affection between
people. Compare the powerful lines of the bird's tail
to the delicate lines of its wings and head.

Plate 35

Plate 36
Design From a Quilt Cover
The branches of a plant are used as a natural
frame within which a flower is seen.

124

Plate 36

Plate 37
Design From a Backcloth Used for Carrying a Baby
The wings of the birds are shaped like those of butterflies.

Plate 37

Plate 38
Design From a Quilt Cover
An open composition where the edge of
the fabric defines the pictorial space, allowing
the design to spread freely and expansively

Plate 38

Plate 39
Design From a Wrapping Cloth
The branches of the plants undulate gently, suggesting
they are under water. The flowing lines also contribute
to the feeling of the fish in the act of swimming.

Plate 39

Plate 40
Design From a Bedsheet
Flowers and buds on curving branches. The bend of the
stems is echoed in the arch of the flying bird's neck.

Plate 40

Plate 41
Design From a Wrapping Cloth (partial view)
Fish, flowers and birds

Plate 41

Plate 42
Design From a Bedsheet
A golden pheasant flying over beautiful flowers.
Dots and circles are unifying elements in the design.

Plate 42   137

Plate 43
Design From a Wrapping Cloth (partial view)
In the center is a round flower surrounded by a diamond
of scalloped curves. A ring of fish surround this, and all
is enclosed by a square border of thin lines and small dots.
This design illustrates the often-used technique of
placing circular designs within square spaces.

Plate 43

Plate 44
Design From a Backcloth Used for Carrying a Baby
Here is a fascinating design of exceptional complexity
and variety. The many borders of dots, zigzags, and
straight and curved lines establish the sense of
pictorial organization and define areas of different
size and shape. The central square encloses several circular
images and is echoed by smaller squares on both sides.
The fish in the outermost band are realistically rendered
compared to the inner ring of stylized fish motifs. The
composition is rich in pattern, movement, rhythm and detail.

Plate 44

Plate 45
Design From the Back of a Coat
A symmetrical design with fish, flowers and birds.
(Note: Illustration suggests effect of ice lines.)

142

Plate 45

DESIGNS FROM
HAUNGPING, GUIZHOU PROVINCE

黄 坪 蜡 染

This section has designs from the Miao people living in the Huangping region in Guizhou province. Huangping is a mountainous forest area full of birds. Thus birds, flowers and flourishing trees constitute the main subjects of the designs. Motifs are often stylized, and the compositions are compact, orderly and carefully balanced.

Plate 46
Design From a Kerchief
Stylized floral motifs are contained within sinuous border lines.
Note the tight composition and the overall balance.

Plate 46

Plate 47
Design From a Waistband
These bird and plant forms are extremely stylized. The emphasis is on decoration and pattern, not natural representation. Compare this design to that of a Miao artist from neighboring Anshun shown in Plate 19.

Plate 47

Plate 48
Design From a Waistband
A lively, compact design of highly stylized motifs.
Note how fish and bird forms are occasionally fused into
a composite image. The fret border around
this gay design is an ancient decorative pattern.

Plate 48

Plate 49
Design From a Wrapping Cloth (partial view)
The central medallion of this dazzling design has a sawtooth
edge, which is repeated within the angular petals of the
large corner flowers. Notice the flowers growing out of
other flowers, suggesting a lush and abundant landscape.
In typical Huangping style, the motifs are geometric and
stylized, and the layout is orderly and balanced.

Plate 49

Plate 50
Design From a Tablecloth (partial view)
At first glance this design appears to emphasize
regularity and order: forceful lines and repeated small semicircles
dominate the design in a formal and methodical way.
But closer inspection reveals dozens of differences in detail,
as if the artist had playfully taken every opportunity
to present us with unexpected variety. This is a delightful example
of one craftwoman's outstanding artistic skill.

Plate 50

Plate 51
Design From a Wrapping Cloth (partial view)
Note the use of triangles and squares
in the structure of the design.

Plate 51

Plate 52
Design From a Wrapping Cloth
Two symmetrical birds and a heart symbolize love
and happiness. (Note: Illustration suggests
effect of ice lines.)

Plate 52

Plate 53
Design From a Waistband
This beautiful, harmonious design uses long
curved lines and stylized bird, flower and fish motifs in regular
repetition. The elegant simplicity of the background
shapes are an important contrast to the rich surface texture
created by the many very short lines. (Note: Illustration
suggests effect of ice lines.)

Plate 53

Plate 54
Design From a Wrapping Cloth
A graceful, flowing and delicate pattern. There are several
floral allusions, but here the focus is on the decorative
quality of the design. The chain of curlicues is remarkable
for its intricacy. (Note: Illustration suggests effect of ice lines.)

Plate 54

DESIGNS FROM DANZHAI, GUIZHOU PROVINCE

丹寨蜡染

This section reproduces batik designs by people of the Miao minority from Danzhai in Guizhou province, an area with many streams and lush river valleys. Birds, flowers, fish and butterflies are common motifs, and peaches and pomegranates are often used for their symbolic significance. The drawings are imaginative and stylized. Compositions tend to be full.

Plate 55
Design From a Kerchief
A fantastic bird with flowers growing out of its
body, and ancillary flower and bird designs

Plate 55

Plate 56
Design From a Teapot Place Mat
Birds and flowers are joined in a lively composition.

Plate 56

Plate 57

Left: Design From a Backcloth Used for Carrying a Baby
Stylized versions of the Chinese character for
"long life," *shou*, are part of a graceful
and unified pattern of peaches and chickens.

Right: Design From a Wrapping Cloth
The layout of this design follows the traditional
method of a central subject and a border pattern.
The flower petals look like fish. Coupled with the
long-life symbols, the design expresses wishes
for longevity and unbounded happiness.

Plate 57

Plate 58
Designs From Quilt Covers
Top: A pomegranate inscribed with the symbol for long
life predicts longevity. Notice how carefully the negative
spaces between the lines have been handled.
Bottom: A peach with the outline of a Chinese coin
expresses the wish for prosperity.

Plate 58

Plate 59
Designs From a Kerchief
Left: Four butterflies, each different from the other,
obscure a flower so that only its top and buds can be seen.
Right: A symmetrical decoration made with thick and
thin lines. The negative spaces of the outermost border
echo the shapes of the inner scalloped frame.

Plate 59

Plate 60
Design From a Backcloth Used for Carrying a Baby
The border is ornamented with *shou* (long life) and *panchang* (endless good fortune) motifs. The central design of flowers and butterflies shows great variety in detail.

Plate 60

Plate 61
Design From a Wrapping Cloth
The regularity of the border scroll acts as a foil for
the irregularity of the varied elements in the central design.
The composition is asymmetrical but well balanced.

Plate 61

Plate 62
Designs From Quilt Covers
Left: A flowerbed with birds on it set in the middle
of a pond of fish. Hold the design upside down and the
fish become fantastic birds with flowers growing out
of them. Right: The butterflies' antennae are
exaggerated for decorative purposes.

Plate 62

Plate 63
Design From a Quilt Cover
Note the stylized birds in the border.

182

Plate 63

Plate 64
Design From a Wrapping Cloth
A busy and unique composition

Plate 64

Plate 65
Miscellaneous Designs From Quilt Covers
These typical Danzhai motifs include
fish, bees and butterflies.

Plate 65

Plate 66
Design From a Kerchief
Each branch bears two kinds of fruit — peaches
and pomegranates — implying longevity for the whole family.
The off-center placement of the major flower motif
gives added interest to the design.

Plate 66

Plate 67
Designs From a Quilt Cover (partial view)
Left: A plant with peaches and an imaginary bird.
Right: Flowers, peaches, birds, and long-life and endless good
fortune symbols express the wish for happiness and
longevity. The large diamond shapes in the center of the design
reappear in miniature in the peaches. A thick, curving
line is used in the central motif and again in the birds' wings.

Plate 67

Plate 68
Designs From Quilt Covers
Left: A fanciful bird. Right: A carefully organized
layout of geometric pomegranates, chickens, fish and flowers.
Exaggeration and distortion of form are characteristic
techniques of the Danzhai, used to enhance the decorative effect.

Plate 68

193

Plate 69
Left: Design From a Quilt Cover
Geometric birds, flowers and insects, symbolizing
unbounded happiness. Note the many
sharp angles in the design.
Right: Design From a Coat Sleeve
The traditional Danzhai *wotuo* design, often used on
coat sleeves and collars is a vibrating pattern,
remarkably dynamic and modern.

194

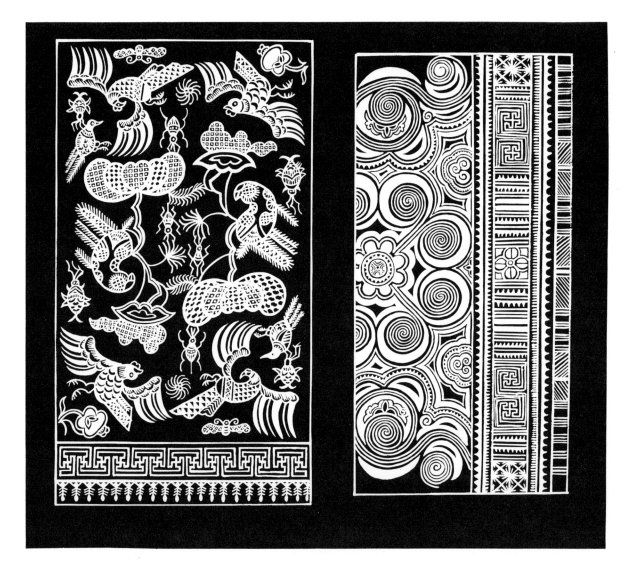

Plate 69

Plate 70
Design From a Kerchief
Fish and butterflies playing with a flower in a lyrical
design that expresses hope for a happy life

196

Plate 70

Plate 71
Design From a Quilt Cover
Here is a design of great vitality. The border
defines an area that is bursting with beating wings; it seems
as if the energy of these birds is impossible to contain.
The powerful, jagged strokes of the wings slice the
space with extraordinary vigor and authority.

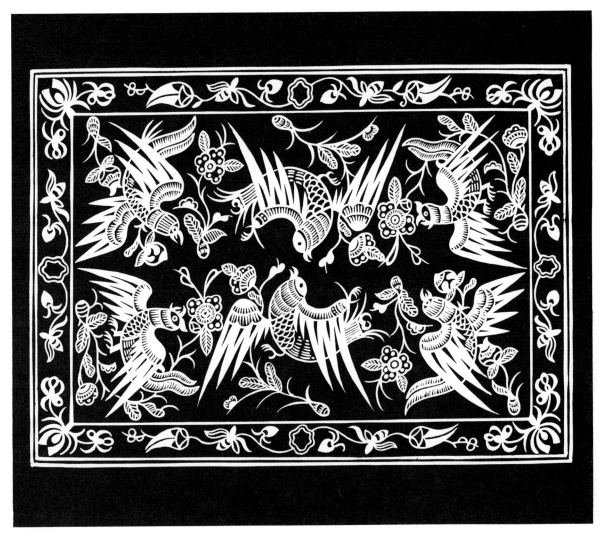

Plate 71

Plate 72
Design From a Wrapping Cloth
Four birds with outstretched wings are flying toward
stylized flowers. The birds are balanced by butterfly motifs.
The composition uses the technique of a round pattern
in a square space. (Note: Illustration suggests effect of ice lines.)

200

Plate 72

Plate 73
Design From a Quilt Cover
Eagles spreading their wings. The image of a sturdy
eagle implies the wish for a strong and healthy boyfriend.
(Note: Illustration suggests effect of ice lines.)

Plate 73

Plate 74
Design From a Backcloth Used for Carrying a Baby
An abundance of children, longevity and wishes for good luck
are symbolized by these designs of peaches, pomegranates and birds.
Danzhai women pay great attention to the symbolic
significance of the designs they used on these backcloths.
(Note: Illustration suggests effect of ice lines.)

Plate 74

Plate 75
Designs From a Wrapping Cloth
Flying eagles. The sharp bills, powerful wings and strong
claws are expressed in a markedly exaggerated and distorted
manner. Compare to figures on the following two pages.
(Note: Illustration suggests effect of ice lines.)

Plate 75

Plate 76
Designs From a Wrapping Cloth
Eagles. (Note: Illustration suggests effect of ice lines.)

Plate 76

Plate 77
Designs From a Wrapping Cloth
Exceptionally beautiful eagle designs. The negative space
between the lines plays an active role in the designs' effectiveness.
(Note: Illustration suggests effect of ice lines.)

Plate 77

DESIGNS FROM
DALI, YUNNAN PROVINCE

大理蜡染

Batik designs by the Yi, Tu and Bai minorities from the Dali district of Yunnan province are shown in this section. The designs exhibit a strong sense of overall pattern. Compositions are varied but stress balance. Repeated floral motifs are common, and images of chickens, horses and cats also appear. In this area the batiks are often combined with embroidery.

213

Plate 78 Yi nationality
Design From an Apron
This design was produced over a century ago.
Two butterflies drawn in different styles are placed opposite
each other. Each is attached to a large flower with
angular petals surrounded by a ring of smaller flowers.
Several flowers appear to be dancing.

Plate 78

Plate 79 Tu nationality
Design From Apron Trimming
A decorative design showing flowers in a continuous line.
Compare to the designs on the following two pages.

Plate 79

Plate 80 Tu nationality
Designs From Apron Trimming
Balanced designs, rich in movement and pattern

Plate 80

Plate 81 Yi nationality
Design From an Apron Trimming (partial view)
The decorative presentation of the cock, with
its abundant feathers and sturdy legs, is an attractive
feature. The stems of the flowers are chains
of the teardrop shape used in the flower on the left.
Both curved and angular border lines appear.

Plate 81

Plate 82 Bai nationality
Design From a Waistband
The design implies happiness and long life.
Note the human figure shown below
the stem of the large flower.

Plate 82

Plate 83 Tu nationality
Design From an Apron
Strong outlines described graceful shapes
within which flowers appear.

Plate 83

Plate 84 Bai nationality
Design From a Child's Cap
Lotuses and peonies, with some flowers taking
the shapes of birds and butterflies.

Plate 84

Plate 85 Tu nationality
Designs From Caps
Top: Peonies Bottom: Fish feeding on flowers

Plate 85

Plate 86 Bai nationality
Designs From a Child's Cap
Flowers and birds

Plate 86

Plate 87 Bai nationality
Designs From Waistbands
A range of imaginative designs. In these examples
we have flowers, butterflies, rats and long-life
symbols, and a child playing with monkeys.

Plate 87

Plate 88 Yi nationality
Designs From Pouches
Left: Birds, flowers and butterflies
Right: A pouch in the shape of a heart with batik designs
and embroidery is a typical present given to a
boyfriend at the time of engagement.

Plate 88

Plate 89 Bai nationality
Designs From Waistbands
These designs incorporate symbols for
happiness and longevity.

Plate 89

Plate 90 Bai nationality
Design From a Backcloth Used for Carrying a Baby
Birds, butterflies and flowers are balanced around a large
peony in a vase inscribed with the Chinese character for joy, *hsi*.
The doubled symbol implies married happiness.

Plate 90

Plate 91 Bai nationality
Design From a Backcloth Used for Carrying a Baby
Domestic pets, poultry and flowers. This design reflects a
courtyard scene. The drawing style is relaxed.

Plate 91

Plate 92 Bai nationality
Designs From Aprons
Branches with many different flowers
symbolize fruitfulness.

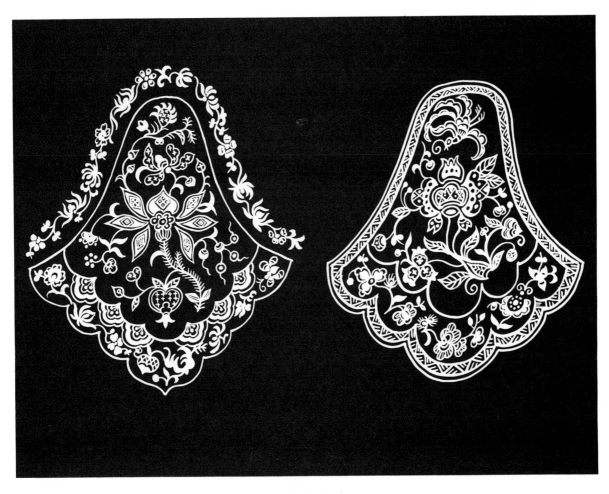

Plate 92

Plate 93 Bai nationality
Designs From Kerchiefs
Flowers, butterflies and birds, drawn in rectangular areas.
The antennae of the butterflies are exaggerated.

Plate 93

Plate 94 Tu nationality
Designs From Apron Trimmings
Note the stylized horses that appear
below the rich floral designs.

Plate 94

Plate 95 Bai nationality
Design From an Apron
Flowers from all four seasons are shown with birds
to symbolize luxuriant growth and prosperity.

Plate 95

Plate 96 Yi nationality
Design From a Backcloth Used for Carrying a Baby
People of the Yi minority live in places where
flowers, chickens, birds and butterflies abound, so naturally
these form the subjects of their batik drawings.
Here, broken lines are used effectively to render the
birds' feathers, and a series of dots suggest the antennae
of the butterfly at the top of the design.

Plate 96

Plate 97 Yi nationality
Design From a Cap
The bird and flower designs on this cap
are perfectly placed to achieve a
rich overall surface texture.

Plate 97

路南蜡染

This section contains batik designs by people of the Yi, Naxi and Miao nationalities of the Lu'nan district in Yunnan province. Yunnan has a subtropical climate and there is great variety in the plant and animal life. This abundance is reflected by the wide range of images that apear in the local batiks: there are flowers, elephants, peacocks, butterflies, sheep, chickens and human figures. Sometimes subjects from regional folk tales are depicted, and sometimes batiks are combined with embroidery.

Plate 98 Yi nationality
Design From a Waistband (partial view)
Flowers placed at regular intervals, linked by a
curving line. The pattern is repeated
on the other side of the band.

256

Plate 98

Plate 99 Yi nationality
Designs From Apron Trimmings
Top: Pomegranates, birds and a cock
Bottom: A symmetrical flower design

Plate 99

Plate 100 Yi nationality
Design From an Apron
Different blossoms grow from a single branch,
implying continuous flowering.
The presentation is orderly and flowing.

Plate 100

Plate 101 Yi nationality
Design From an Apron
Note the prominent butterfly, and the bold, wide lines.

Plate 101

Plate 102 Yi nationality
Design From a Backcloth Used for Carrying a Baby
This asymmetrical, open design expresses wishes for a happy life
and a good future for the child. There is an unusual
robed figure to the left of the central flower.

Plate 102

Plate 103 Miao nationality
Designs From Dress Material
Top: Bands of geometric shapes surround stylized flowers.
Bottom: A balanced design of poultry and peonies

Plate 103

Plate 104 Yi nationality
Designs From a Backcloth (partial view)
Left: A balanced floral composition
Right: Miscellaneous motifs

Plate 104

Plate 105 Yi nationality
Design From Sleeve Trimming
Long, thin lines and unadorned background space
give these designs an open, airy quality.

Plate 105

Plate 106 Yi nationality
Top: Design From a Woman's Cap
Bottom: Design From a Woman's Waistband
Chickens, sheep, fish, flowers and human figures drawn
with considerable distortion and exaggeration

Plate 106

Plate 107 Yi nationality
Design From a Teapot Place Mat
A golden pheasant spreads its wings in this elegant design.
The lacy border adds to the feeling of refinement.

Plate 107

Plate 108 Yi nationality
Design From a Backpack
Flowers and a semicircular border of traditional
fret and endless-good-fortune ornaments

Plate 108

Plate 109 Naxi nationality
Designs From Dress Material
Double elephants, peacocks and a butterfly

Plate 109

Plate 110 Yi nationality
Left: Design From a Kerchief (partial view)
Butterflies and flying peacocks. Stylized flowers form border patterns.

Right: Miscellaneous Flower Design
A sturdy flower with a curved stem being
approached by butterflies

Plate 110

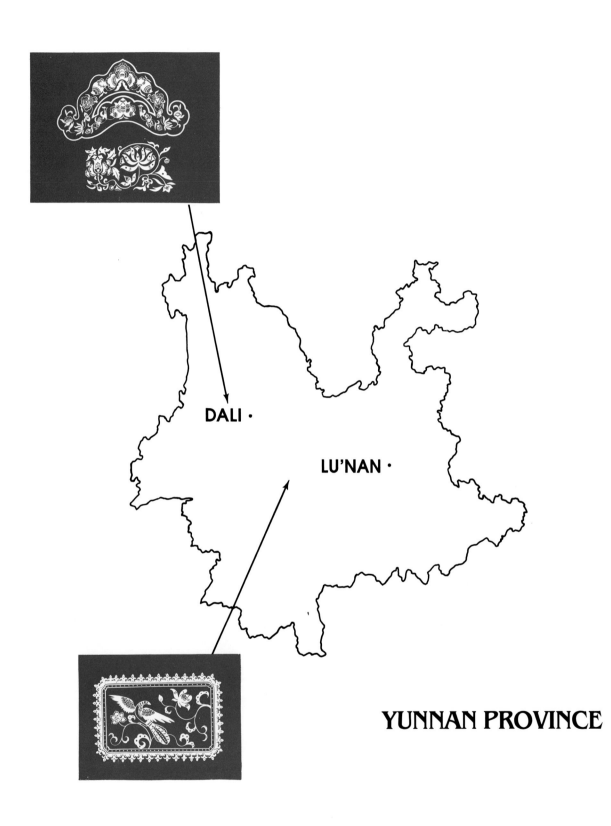

DALI ·

LU'NAN ·

YUNNAN PROVINCE

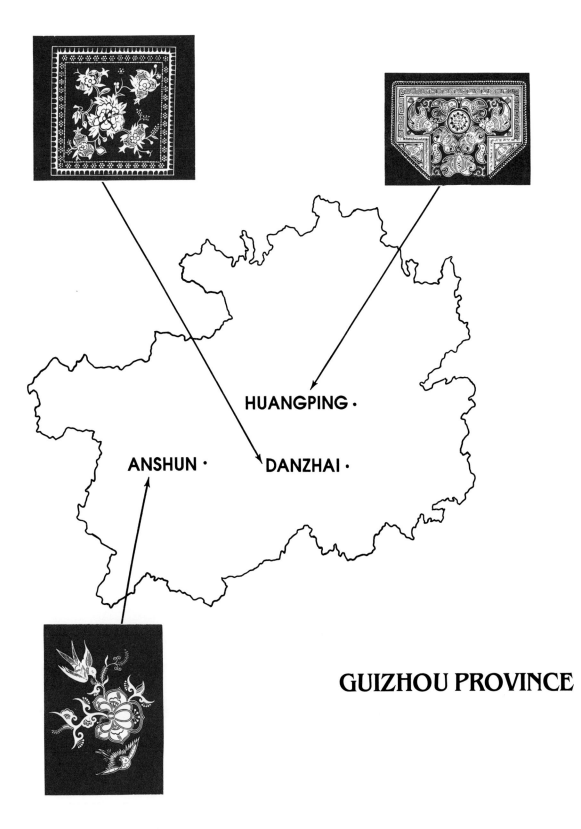

HUANGPING ·

ANSHUN ·   DANZHAI ·

GUIZHOU PROVINCE